Muse in a Suitcase

Muse in a Suitcase

Poems by

Charise M. Hoge

Cover design by Shay Culligan
Cover art by Sandra Guiloff

ISBN: 978-1-954353-25-1

Kelsay Books
502 South 1040 East, A-119
American Fork, Utah 84003

For
the journey
to a poem

Acknowledgments

Grateful acknowledgment is made to the editors of the following publications where these poems first appeared:

Journal of Military Experience & the Arts: "French Kiss"
Next Line, Please: Prompts to Inspire Poets and Writers (David Lehman, Cornell University Press): "Uluru"
The American Scholar "Next Line, Please" poetry column: "Wayfarer," "Long Story Short," "Daresay," "Vacation, Italy," "Shakespeare and Company," "Morocco," "Aphorismic"
The New Verse News: "For the Rohingya"
Tiny Seed Literary Journal: "On the Porch"
Ulalume Journal: "Eating Nasturtiums"

For the gift of a writing community, my gratitude goes to the poets of "Next Line, Please" and the Capitol Hill Poetry Group.

For sharing her artistic vision, my heartfelt thanks to Sandra Guiloff, the cover artist.

And for being the first reader of all my poems, thanks many times over to my husband, Charles.

Contents

Wayfarer

women walking prayers
weaving to the Western Wall
wallpapering like wisteria
willing, willing, willing
beflowering woefulness
witnesses windowless
—while less than half, their piece
unequal to the men's side—
women wait, accommodate,
weigh words, and waist by waist
wedge into stone to scale
a way where peace is with

French Kiss

Absence is not absinthe,
though it offers a heady whiff
of intoxication.

You arrive in camouflage.
The first hug is relief
peppered with roadblocks

—the near hit, constant heat.
You're wooden as a crate
of goods, the scavenging of war.

I'll bargain on seduction's truce
to pry you through your pores.
We'll lip-sync whatever's missing.

Frail April, Notre-Dame

St. Geneviève of the spire,
we do not deny our tendency
to crumble, the ash we are while
breathing, the spine that isn't fixed,
made of knotty vertebrae, the patella
of our knees weakening, without patina.
We do not deny what transpires in hours
of ages, the ghost of an exclamation point,
awe that goes before and after, our rawness.

Shakespeare and Company

I knew you when
nothing was trending
in a world without a wide web.
Nigh overhead a cobweb
dallies in your cathedral of books.
Windows the river Seine overlook
—still—how I rushed in the rain
homesick, an American
in Paris sans Gershwin's score.
You opened your door.
A beacon in a city of light when
I was twenty and reticent.
We needed no music, no café
for rendezvous; it was how you say
"read me" "come upstairs"
"forget the time," as though you cared.

Ode to the Big Tomato

Two blocks along
the Rue de Seine
we shop by the half kilo
for salad ingredients
to toss together
in the closet-size kitchen
of our pied-à-terre
with tall windows
wide open to the street
one flight of stairs above
cars bumping gently
back and forth
to parallel park;
I ask for a baguette
while Anita buys
the first tomatoes,
a food I didn't eat—
devoid of flavor at my local
supermarket—but here
in the sixth arrondissement
where we study history, urban
planning, French literature and
parlance, in this city where
we choose to spend our junior year
abroad, I gain from a tomato
the revelation of taste.

Sonnet for a Statue, Wall Street

She’s not a bullfighter,
may have lived next door
or once your daughter.
“Fearless Girl” has no score
to settle, but a stance
sorely familiar as if always
defining defiance
of bullies who raise
backs spineless never
ask permission to rig
the skies or monopolize terra
firma. Formidable, she can dig
into her burgeoning being,
like a star from nebula freeing.

Hotel Eternity

Get me a room at Hotel Eternity
—Charles Simic

Where the bed is laden
white with geese,
a crystalline lake underneath,
the imponderability of place.

A window half-shut
or partly open,

the wind on a crescendo of
arising or subsiding,

a rocking chair.

In the in-between
it's surprisingly clear
that the status quo
has direction.

If I pick up your used dish to rinse
you won't look back
and you will not think of me.

Eating Nasturtiums

Peppery bloomskins make me salivate
—orange taste uncitrus—rambunctious
unlike inedible ranunculus—zing
surprising—reminiscent of salted dried
plums from the Chinese market, La Cresta,
in the sweat of Panama City—keeping
the seed tucked into my inner cheek
long after sucking the gnarly fruitmeat
—only once downing the rocklike
remnant while tying my shoes for the first
time—reassured that it would pass through
me—that we discard the wrong material
—we are made to be revised.

Long Story Short

Some resolutions rise
like fireworks…showy,
bright, dissipating.
What of the resolve
to be precisely here—
New Year's Eve on a
terrace overlooking
the Pacific, my father's clasp
around my shoulders
(his quiet ardor apparent
as an undertow)?
This Mississippi man
whose fluent Spanish has
a southern twang, who began
in a shotgun house and found
Panama a homeland. I see his naps;
ask for tales of escapades:
Bolivia, Venezuela, Singapore,
a diverted landing in Tashkent
to live in an airport for three days.
He's 112 pounds, as if accumulation
of risk has cut to the firebrand marrow.
Shuffling in flip-flops, with
his sagas fastened to his frame.

Daresay

Be it pluck or luck, of Irish
descent a Catholic sits,
not on ceremony,
but knee to knee
at a Hindu temple—hive that thrums,
saris that sway to the call, the drum.
Old woman in saffron stands to dance,
wide the drummer's smile, jubilate in chants.
Every body is a celebrant. Name heresy
for what it is, a lonely frock of hearsay.

Letter from Bundi City

If you were still standing
in your Southern kitchen
cooking okra you had sliced
and coated with corn meal,
I would tell you that in India
they prepare them whole,
called ladyfingers,
at this rooftop café
wrapped by barbed wire
to keep the monkeys at bay.

There's a view of the palace
and few visitors
to these ruins of grandeur,
yet someone sprinkled red
rose petals on the marble throne;
and a flock of schoolchildren
press and plead for my autograph,
as if any foreign blond be praised.

It's best to walk behind a cow
that is divinely carefree
like your great-granddaughters
(there are two now),
as motorbikes whiz past shops
with colorful cloth to sell.
And I would tell you thanks
for the patchwork quilt
you nearly finished sewing.

For the Rohingya

There are some
who must turn fire
into a tidal wave,
become a waterfall
mountain cascade.
But they are not liquid
made. Sinewy and limbed,
in limbo a long walk
from any land with their name,
where any can say "mine."
"Mine" becomes the casualty
of forwardness, of egress.
Damages damming arrival
of a people—unchampioned,
already damned.

Uluru

Undone by trial of trail cresting full sun.
Letters approach incantation chasm imaginative.
Underfoot red dirt decorates hem, cakes tread of soles.
Rim of rock, circling the ancestors' wholly baked faith:
Understand your walk alone, al-one, is all one.

The Way

The way she moves, it's beautiful.
Ankle bells tell rotation of feet
while hips accent left to rightful,
elbows exalt into the downbeat.
A continuity of snaking arms greets
bangles that jangle in a new refrain
as her head slides west to east.
Shoulders shimmy like rain
shimmering through human frame;
she may captivate she will not pay
ransom owed to an ancient claim.
It's she who moves the way
—like a divining rod
recalls the beautiful on arid sod.

Summer Folio

To nature a city of olive trees
is born…overarching like parasols
against the rays of infinite sayings
that die behind the teeth,
that religion doesn't save or explain.
Quickly time trembles.
Two questions stand like mountain
peaks overlooking the sea.
Spill of foothills offers foliage,
a pergola and a bench. Reminiscence
translated as scenic postcards.

Morocco

You're a muscle memory
yet to be acquired, a taste
well-known—of tagine and harissa.
How I miss you when we haven't met.
See your lantern lit in my library.

Adams Morgan is a pseudo-souk
—I'm sold on a pair of your babouche.
Impractical footwear gets me nowhere
near a medina, but shuttles after quaint.
These bids to make your acquaintance,
see? Your lantern lit in my library.

Venice

For a tourist walking a map
believing in a destination
maze of cobblestone lures and traps
for a tourist walking a map
short film of masks, tassels, glass wraps
into kaleidoscopic friction
for a tourist walking a map
believing in a destination

Vacation, Italy

Fancy a purse, find of a holiday.
Oh daily peruse of linings of gold,
of yellow silk. Well yolk is more my color,
sunny side up, dawn.

We wake to hike in the Dolomites.
By evening, learn "vives!" for cheers,
unblinking. It goes to my head; toes go
tickling effervescence of us.
The contents of many an anniversary
carried light.

Speechless

The One Thing That Can Save America
—John Ashbery

Let's go back to zero—
no savoir faire, savior, hero.
The great ideas won't accumulate
on banks, mountains, vales, or lakes.
Any stake in shores of sure—verboten.
Where "oh" is the only language spoken.
This urge to laugh without knowing
what our joke is—it comes like lightning
to the table, as we sit like star-crossed mates.
A cackle that chimes across the setting of plates.

Orange Vest

On an old shale logging road
we cross one stream, another,
farther and farther

stirring our own sap upward,
sluggish, we meander on instinct,
pick up the pace in our woods

we've walked over and over
a hundred acres is what it takes
to lose track of what infiltrates

headlines of papers and posts;
we pass the remnant of a fence
rubble mound of a cairn

on a slope of land an echo
away from hunters domain
our dominion ribboned in

rays that splinter through trees,
we proceed vested as human-
kind to remind we are not prey

Bray

...the old bray of my heart. I am. I am. I am.
—Sylvia Plath

Bravura, blush of heat,
flush of hearts in a crooked game,
notes of shame, rage without
a red carpet—across the crimson
highway she's driving
a point home. She is. She is.

Bridge traversed tilts backward.
Rights disputed, miles reversed.

Pale porcelain damsel
demure squeaking coquettish,
petite feet cinched waist…faints,
wakes flummoxed. She is
an icon in a century gone caesura.

Commuter Pew

On the church marquee:
  "The Gospel According to Moss."
Doctrine softens…breathes…
on the church marquee
marking the circle, Maryland to D.C.
Cars at a caterpillar crawl in morning rush.
On the church marquee:
  "The Gospel According to Moss."

Aphorismic

When a door closes, there
was never a door. Or,
I could be wrong.

In Thailand it’s bad luck
to step squarely
onto thresholds—even
with shoes removed.

Be aware of a crossroads
to enter a place—
leave the rubble of the road
and go unlaced, eyelets
with their strings attached
left on the stoop.

Upon return,
check for small frogs nestled
in footbeds.
Make no assumption
that things are as they have been.

Flow

backward is wolf
is fur is tracks is dirt
of grasses of lawns
with signs “hate has
no home here”
with sighs of willows
will, oh will we know
neighbors born of
family trees deforested
of stories hoarded
not to end but to bend
into wind whipping
a whip-poor-will
calls a repeated refrain
to cry its name
the ten thousand things
are one and the
same word
forward is flow

Sandpaper

It's the particulars of a mosaic
in the curve of an archway
Entering Marrakesh, the driver frets
over a decree to wear gloves

It's the curl of mint in a glass
for a welcome pour of hospitality
Vendors lose interest in hawking wares,
looking at their phones

It's the pervasive smell of orange blossom
from a sunken grove of trees
In the palace courtyard there are a few wandering
tourists and feral cats

It's the intervals of a call to prayer
...morning, afternoon, evening...
Five times over the course of a day,
filling the air with constancy

Royal Air Maroc cancels our flight,
suggests a reservation for next month
It's the songs of the Sahara released
into the night, beneath a flood of stars

All international flights to and from
the kingdom of Morocco are suspended
It's the rugged structure of an ancient Kasbah,
the splendor of an interior room

We plead at our embassy's door,
while Europeans are booked on charter flights
It's the orbs of angel's trumpet at the Riad
we flee…for a chance to get on board

On the Porch

He who kisses the joy as it flies
—William Blake

August.
At the behest
of nature, life feels epiphanous.

In the simultaneous
lazy, longevity grows slender.
Thick with humid blooms, summer's

bound to shift. I swoon over
this butterfly—suddenly my worst fear
lacks reason to exist—
as it lights upon these sighing lips.

About the Author

Charise M. Hoge is a dance/movement therapist, writer, and performing artist. She is a graduate of Sarah Lawrence College (BA), New York University (MA), and University of Georgia (MSW). Her work in arts and healing has brought wellness programs into hospitals, counseling centers, Smithsonian museums, and businesses. She is co-author of *A Portable Identity: A Woman's Guide to Maintaining a Sense of Self While Moving Overseas* and author of the chapbook *Striking Light from Ashes.* Her poetry is also featured in *Next Line, Please: Prompts to Inspire Poets and Writers* (Cornell University Press, 2018), as well as various journals and magazines. Charise has given poetry readings at a variety of venues, including a moving streetcar for Art All Night DC.

www.ingramcontent.com/pod-product-compliance
Lightning Source LLC
LaVergne TN
LVHW020050110826
845155LV00029B/711

* 9 7 8 1 9 5 4 3 5 3 2 5 1 *